W9-BDK-970

2

HORSING AROUND

SHOW HORSES

By Laura Loria

Gareth Stevens
Publishing

Please visit our Web site, www.garethstevens.com. For a free color catalog of all our high-quality books, call toll free 1-800-542-2595 or fax 1-877-542-2596.

Library of Congress Cataloging-in-Publication Data

Loria, Laura.
  Show horses / Laura Loria.
      p. cm. – (Horsing around)
  Includes index.
  ISBN 978-1-4339-4640-0 (pbk.)
  ISBN 978-1-4339-4641-7 (6-pack)
  ISBN 978-1-4339-4639-4 (library binding)
  1. Show horses. 2. Horse shows. I. Title.
  SF295.185.F49 2007
  798.2'4–dc22

                                          2010030120

First Edition

Published in 2011 by
Gareth Stevens Publishing
111 East 14th Street, Suite 349
New York, NY 10003

Copyright © 2011 Gareth Stevens Publishing

Designer: Michael J. Flynn
Editor: Therese Shea

Photo credits: Cover, p. 1, (cover, back cover, p. 1 wooden sign), (pp. 2–4, 6, 9, 11–12, 14–18, 20–24 wood background), back cover (wood background), pp. 5, 7, 8, 16, 20 Shutterstock.com; pp. 10–11 Jamie McDonald/Getty Images; p. 13 Julian Herbert/ Getty Images; p. 15 Tim Platt/Iconica/Getty Images; p. 19 iStockphoto.com.

Printed in the United States of America

CPSIA compliance information: Batch #CW11GS: For further information contact Gareth Stevens, New York, New York at 1-800-542-2595.

Contents

Words in the glossary appear in **bold** type the first time they are used in the text.

Different Horses for Different Shows

Every type of horse, or **breed**, is known for certain features. Appaloosas are good jumpers. Arabian horses can run fast over long distances. The Trakhener breed is known for following orders. For speed, few horses can beat a Thoroughbred or a quarter horse. Morgans are used for nearly every event! There are many more talented breeds. Almost any horse can be a show horse. You just have to find the kind of show that matches the horse's talents.

THE MANE FACT

All Thoroughbred horses have the same birthday—January 1! They aren't all born on this day, but having one date makes it easy to keep records on Thoroughbreds.

Some horses are naturally good jumpers. They still need to train for shows.

Western Riding

The Western style of riding began with cowboys. They needed horses to obey commands as they looked after livestock. Western horse shows test similar skills.

The Western-style rider holds the horse's **reins** loosely in one hand. The rider places the reins on the horse's neck to tell it where to go. Riders also give directions by changing position in the saddle and using their legs. Walking is the horse's slowest movement, followed by **trotting**. **Cantering** is faster, and **galloping** is the fastest movement.

THE MANE FACT

Why do Western riders use only one hand on the reins? Because cowboys needed the other hand free to rope cattle!

The Western saddle, or leather seat, is comfortable for sitting for long periods of time.

Many roping events are completed in just seconds!

THE MANE FACT

In a penning event, a horse and rider separate a calf from a herd and put it into a small pen.

Western Events

In Western horse shows, there are different events. Reining requires the horse and rider to complete a pattern of movements decided by the judges. There also may be a "reining back" test. During this, the rider stops a galloping horse in an instant.

In pleasure events, show horses make it look as if they're just out for a ride. Judges call out different speeds. Riders must make their horses follow their orders, while looking as if they're not giving orders! Judges decide if a horse looks like a "pleasure" to ride.

Holding the horse's reins tight, this English rider can turn in a tight corner.

English Riding

The other style of riding is known as English riding. It's been practiced for centuries. Unlike the Western saddle, the English saddle weighs little and is flat. It's not as easy to stay on and sit straight.

The main difference between English and Western riding is that the English rider holds the reins in both hands to control the horse. The rider pulls on the horse's reins with more force and keeps them tight.

THE MANE FACT

In the past, women had to ride sidesaddle—with both legs on one side of the horse. Now, sidesaddle riding is a special event in horse shows.

English Events

Some events in English riding shows are similar to Western show events. Like the Western pleasure event, a **dressage** event is about a rider making their horse follow a pattern of commands. However, movements are much slower and more exact.

Endurance events are races that may be up to 100 miles (160 km) long. Jumper and hunting events involve horses and riders leaping over **obstacles** on a course. Riders lose points if a horse knocks over—or even touches—a fence.

"Anky" van Grunsven of the Netherlands won the dressage gold medal at the 2000, 2004, and 2008 Olympics.

Dress and Grooming

In horse shows, both horse and rider are given points on how they look! A Western show rider's clothing includes boots, long pants, and a hat. Some people wear cowboy hats. Others wear helmets. Western riders may wear **chaps** like real cowboys! English-style dress is more fancy, with hunting caps, fitted jackets, tall boots, and **jodhpurs** (JAHD-puhrz).

A show horse needs to look even better. The horse should be groomed, or cleaned and brushed. Special attention should be given to its hoofs. Sometimes the mane and tail are braided.

THE MANE FACT

Some horse shows have a fancy-dress event. The rider wears a costume. Sometimes the horse does, too!

Gloves are often worn
in dressage events.

15

The reins and bridle help the rider "talk" to the horse.

"Tack" is the word for the things worn by a horse so it can be ridden. All show horses have a saddle, bridle, reins, and bit. Each saddle is specially made for the horse's body. It is oiled to stay soft. The bridle is the set of leather straps that go around the horse's head. The bit is the mouthpiece attached to the bridle and reins. When the rider pulls on the reins, the bit presses on the horse's mouth or nose. This tells the horse to move a certain direction.

THE MANE FACT

In horse shows, the horse and rider should wear similar colors to get more points.

Traveling with horses to shows isn't easy! When packing for a horse show, it's best to be prepared for anything. While in its trailer, the horse should wear a blanket. Leg and tail wraps help keep it clean.

Other items to pack are grooming tools, buckets, hay for bedding, and grain for feeding. There are different kinds of coverings to bring to the show, such as those that keep off flies, rain, and the cold. A comfortable horse will perform well.

When traveling long distances, a horse should be offered food and drink every 2 to 4 hours.

How does a rider begin showing horses? Many local shows offer beginning riders a chance to help out. They can learn how a show works before they enter one. Local shows are the best way to start out in the horse-show world.

After riders gain experience, they move on to **regional** shows. At this level, the horse and rider may need a trainer to help them improve. Finally, the rider and horse may be able to move on to national shows!

Features of a Show Horse

Motion	should seem relaxed with a powerful backside and a high front
Neck	long and somewhat upright
Head	small with large eyes, small ears, and a straight nose
Back	short and somewhat level; well-shaped shoulders
Legs	long with well-formed bones
Tail	high and flowing

THE MANE FACT

"Equestrian" means horseback rider or horseback riding.

Glossary

breed: a group of animals that share features different from others of that kind

canter: a smooth way of moving for a horse, slower than a gallop but faster than a trot

chaps: leggings made of leather that are worn over pants

dressage: an event in which a horse and rider are judged on the horse's movements

endurance: the power to do something hard for a long time

gallop: the fastest running movement for a horse

jodhpurs: riding pants that are wide at the hip and narrow below the knee

obstacle: something that blocks a path

regional: belonging to a certain area

reins: straps for controlling a horse

trot: a horse's movement that is faster than walking but slower than running

For More Information

Books:

Fetty, Margaret. *Show Horses*. New York, NY: Bearport Publishing, 2007.

Johnson, Robin R. *Show Jumping*. New York, NY: Crabtree Publishing Company, 2009.

Kimball, Cheryl. *Horse Showing for Kids*. North Adams, MA: Storey Kids, 2004.

Web Sites:

The Canadian Pony Club FUN! Pages
www.canadianponyclub.org/Misc/Games/
Read stories about horses, and take a horse quiz.

Pony Club Games and Puzzles
i-uspc.org/games/
Play games while learning about grooming, bridles, and saddles.

Index